I0606086

THIS IS THE ONLY BOOK OF DAD JOKES YOU'LL EVER NEED

THIS IS THE ONLY BOOK OF DAD JOKES YOU'LL EVER NEED

302 of the Best and Most Cringeworthy Dad Jokes

EDITED BY THOMAS NOWAK
ILLUSTRATED BY ALBERTO MIRANDA

CHRONICLE BOOKS
SAN FRANCISCO

Library of Congress Cataloging-in-Publication Data available.

ISBN 978-1-7972-4176-0

Manufactured in China.

Design by Maggie Edelman.
Illustrations by Alberto Miranda.

10 9 8 7 6 5 4 3 2 1

Chronicle books and gifts are available at special quantity discounts to corporations, professional associations, literacy programs, and other organizations. For details and discount information, please contact our premiums department at corporategifts@chroniclebooks.com or at 1-800-759-0190.

Chronicle Books LLC
680 Second Street
San Francisco, California 94107
www.chroniclebooks.com

FOR ALL THE DADS
WHO NEVER GIVE UP TRYING
TO GET A LAUGH

(EVEN WHEN THEY SHOULD)

CONTENTS

Chapter 1

MASTER OF THE GRILL, WITH A SIDE OF CORNY QUIPS

HOW MANY APPLES
GROW ON A TREE?

ALL OF THEM.

SHOULD I GRILL THE CHICKEN BREASTS OR THE THIGHS?

I THINK I'LL JUST WING IT!

WHY DIDN'T THE TURKEY WANT MORE MASHED POTATOES?

IT WAS STUFFED!

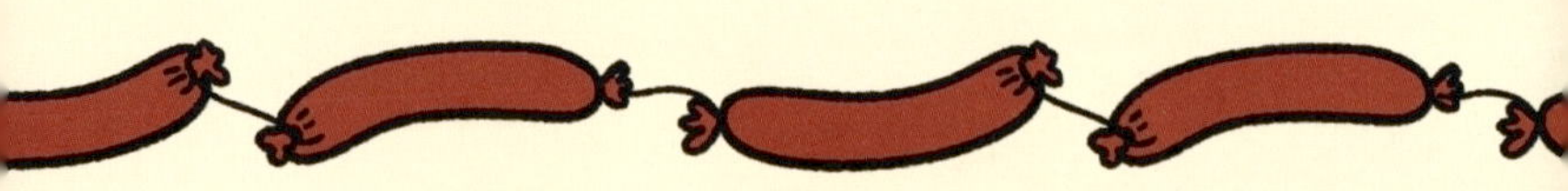

MOM: "WHY DIDN'T YOU SEASON THE MEAT?"

DAD: "I RAN OUT OF THYME."

I HAD A DATE LAST NIGHT,
AND IT WAS PERFECT.

TOMORROW, I'LL HAVE A FIG.

MY WIFE ASKED ME TO GO GET SIX CANS OF SPRITE FROM THE GROCERY STORE.

I REALIZED WHEN I GOT HOME THAT I HAD PICKED SEVEN UP.

WHICH STATE HAS THE SMALLEST SOFT DRINKS?

MINNESOTA.

WHAT DANCE DO CHEESEMAKERS DO ON HALLOWEEN?

THE MUENSTER MASH.

I ASKED OUR PRIEST
TO BLESS AN AVOCADO.

NOW WE HAVE
HOLY GUACAMOLE.

WHAT DID THE PASTA WHO WAS LOCKED OUT OF HIS HOUSE SAY?

"I HAVE GNOCCHI."

WHAT DO YOU CALL ZOMBIES WHO ONLY COOK BRAINS IN WOKS?

THE WOKING DEAD.

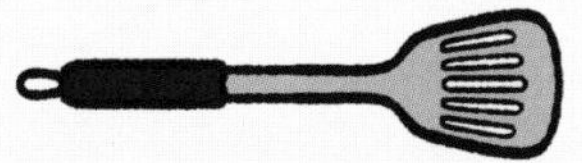

YESTERDAY, I ACCIDENTALLY SWALLOWED TOO MUCH FOOD COLORING.

I FEEL LIKE I DYED A LITTLE INSIDE.

WHY DON'T EGGS
TELL JOKES?

THEY'D CRACK EACH
OTHER UP.

I WAS GOING TO SAVE
MY LEFTOVERS FOR TOMORROW
NIGHT, BUT I FORGOT.

MY PLANS WERE FOILED.

I HEARD A SONG ABOUT A TORTILLA.

IT WAS A NICE WRAP.

DID YOU HEAR ABOUT
THE ELDERLY NOODLE CHEF?

HE PASTA WAY.

WHAT HAPPENS BEFORE
IT RAINS CANDY?

IT SPRINKLES.

I WAS GOING TO BET $100
I COULD REACH THE
STEAKS ON THE TOP SHELF
OF THE REFRIGERATOR.

THEN I REALIZED THE
STEAKS WERE TOO HIGH.

WHAT'S A CHICKEN'S LEAST FAVORITE DAY OF THE WEEK?

FRY DAY.

WHY DID THE BANANA
GO TO THE DOCTOR?

BECAUSE IT WASN'T
PEELING WELL.

WHY CAN'T YOU TRUST BURRITOS?

THEY TEND TO SPILL THE BEANS.

MY WIFE USES A KITCHEN TOOL TO SHRED GARLIC AND BLUE CHEESE, BOTH OF WHICH I HATE.

IT REALLY IS THE GRATER OF TWO EVILS.

MY FRIEND AND I OPENED A RESTAURANT TOGETHER.

I GUESS THAT MAKES US TASTE BUDS.

WHY DID THE
SALTSHAKER GO TO JAIL?

FOR A-SALT WITH
A DEADLY WEAPON.

WHY DID THE PICKLE GET SPECIAL TREATMENT?

BECAUSE HE'S KIND OF A BIG DILL.

WHAT DO YOU CALL A NOODLE THAT'S A STRANGER?

ONE THAT UDON KNOW.

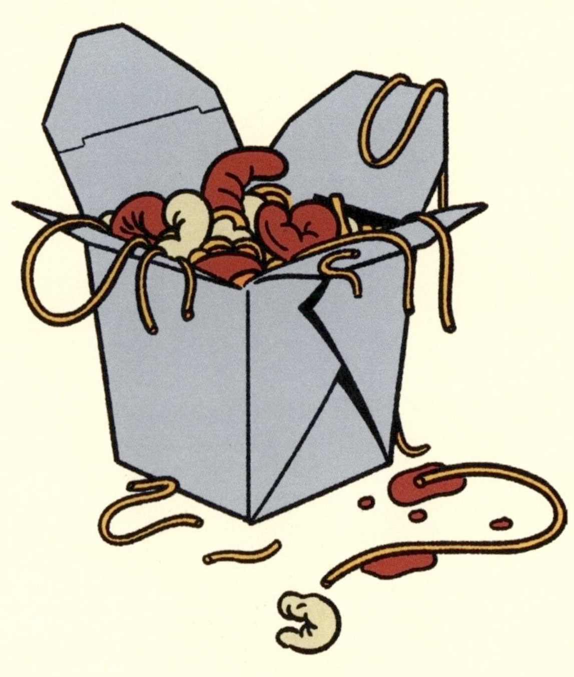

WHAT KIND OF FOOD DO KILLER WHALES SERVE AT COCKTAIL PARTIES?

SHARKUTERIE.

FRIED SHRIMP ARE ALWAYS ANGRY.

THEY HAVE A HARD TIME CONTROLLING THEIR TEMPURA.

DUMPLINGS ARE NEVER SATISFIED.

THEY'RE ALWAYS LEFT WONTON MORE.

WHICH MOLLUSK IS THE MOST IN SHAPE?

MUSSELS.

WHAT DID ONE PLATE SAY TO THE OTHER PLATE?

"DINNER'S ON ME!"

WHY WAS THE ICE CREAM CONE SUCH A GOOD REPORTER?

IT ALWAYS GOT THE SCOOP.

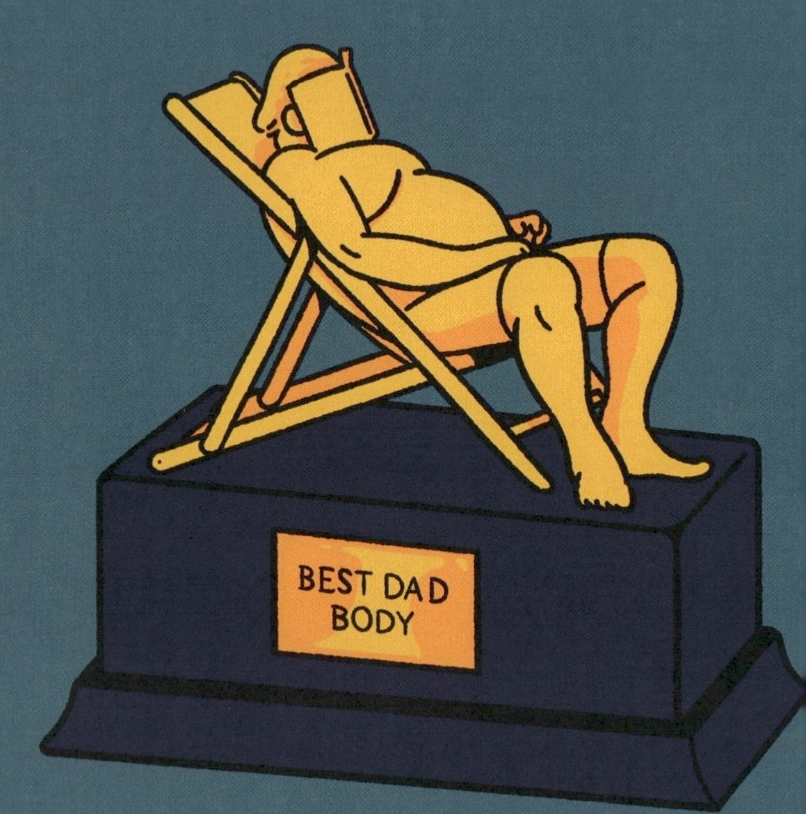
BEST DAD
BODY

Chapter 2

THE DAD BOD IS HERE

MY SIX-PACK IS VERY
PRECIOUS TO ME.

THAT'S WHY I PROTECT IT
WITH A LAYER OF FAT.

WHAT KIND OF EXERCISE
IS PERFECT FOR LAZY PEOPLE?

DIDDLY SQUATS!

SOME PEOPLE SAY I
HAVE A DAD BOD, BUT I
LIKE TO THINK OF IT
AS A FATHER FIGURE.

MY LOCAL GYM COSTS $120 FOR AN ENTIRE YEAR. THAT'S $60 PER VISIT; NOT A GREAT DEAL!

WHAT DO YOU CALL
SOMEONE WHO WON'T STICK
TO A DIET?

A DESSERTER.

WHY AM I SO TIRED
ON APRIL 1?

I JUST FINISHED A
THIRTY-ONE-DAY MARCH.

WHEN PEOPLE ASK IF I EXERCISE, I TELL THEM I DO CRUNCHES EVERY DAY.

CAP'N CRUNCH, CINNAMON TOAST CRUNCH, NESTLÉ CRUNCH . . .

DID YOU HEAR ABOUT
THE WEIGHT LIFTER WHO GOT
KICKED OUT OF HIS HOUSE?

HE WAS SQUATTING.

WHAT DID THE WEIGHT LIFTER
SAY WHEN HE OPENED
HIS TUB OF PROTEIN POWDER?

"NO WHEY!"

DAD: "DOCTOR, MY STOMACH IS GETTING REALLY BIG."

DOCTOR: "YOU SHOULD DIET."

DAD: "WHAT COLOR?"

I THOUGHT THE
DRYER WAS SHRINKING
MY CLOTHES.

TURNS OUT IT WAS
THE REFRIGERATOR!

I'M THE CHAMPION
OF RELAXING.

MY DOCTOR TOLD ME IF
I CONTINUE BEING INACTIVE,
I CAN EXPECT ATROPHY.

WIFE: "IF YOU WANT TO GET IN SHAPE, YOU SHOULD START CLIMBING STAIRS."

HUSBAND: "I'M NOT SURE WHERE TO EVEN START. I'D NEED A STEP-BY-STEP GUIDE."

I SAW THE WEIRDEST THING AT THE GYM THE OTHER DAY. THIS GUY ON THE TREADMILL PUT A WATER BOTTLE IN THE PRINGLES CAN HOLDER.

I RECENTLY SWITCHED
MY SCALE FROM
POUNDS TO KILOGRAMS.

IT CREATED
MASS CONFUSION.

EVERY MORNING, I TELL MY
PARTNER THAT I'M GOING TO JOG
AROUND THE NEIGHBORHOOD,
BUT I NEVER DO.

IT'S A RUNNING JOKE WE HAVE.

I WANT TO GO ON A DIET,
BUT I JUST HAVE TOO MUCH
ON MY PLATE RIGHT NOW.

WHAT'S THE BEST WAY
TO BURN 1,000 CALORIES?

LEAVE THE PIZZA IN THE OVEN.

I ASKED MY DATE TO MEET
ME AT THE GYM,
BUT SHE NEVER SHOWED UP.

I GUESS THE TWO OF US
AREN'T GOING TO WORK OUT.

WHAT GOES UP BUT
NEVER COMES DOWN?

MY WEIGHT.

SOME PEOPLE SAY
WEIGHT IS ONLY A NUMBER,
BUT THAT'S ABSURD.

WEIGHT IS CLEARLY A WORD.

DIETING IS A MATTER OF WILLPOWER.

A TRIUMPH OF MIND OVER PLATTER.

HOW DO YOU QUICKLY WEIGH A MILLENNIAL DAD?

IN INSTAGRAMS.

WHAT'S HARDER TO CATCH
THE FASTER YOU RUN?

YOUR BREATH.

I'M INTO FITNESS.

FIT'N'ESS PIZZA
INTO MY MOUTH!

MY ABS REFUSE
TO DO SIT-UPS.

THEY DON'T LIKE GETTING
BENT OUT OF SHAPE.

WHAT DID THE CHEESE
SAY TO HIS WORKOUT BUDDY?

"BRO, YOU'RE SHREDDED!"

MY FAVORITE EXERCISE
IS A CROSS BETWEEN
A LUNGE AND A CRUNCH.

I CALL IT *LUNCH*.

MY SON SAID HE WAS GOING TO THE GYM TO LIFT.

I REPLIED, "NOW, THAT'S A WEIGHTY DECISION!"

I RUN RELIGIOUSLY.

ABOUT ONCE OR TWICE AROUND THE HOLIDAYS.

THE TREADMILL AND I HAVE A LOVE-HATE RELATIONSHIP.

IT LOVES TO RUN, AND I HATE TO RUN.

THERE WAS A NEW MACHINE AT THE GYM TODAY. IT'S REALLY INTENSE—I USED IT FOR AN HOUR AND FELT SICK.

IT'S GREAT, THOUGH; IT'S GOT EVERYTHING: KIT KAT BARS, M&M'S, SNICKERS, THE LOT!

Chapter 3

ONLY DADS IN THE AUDIENCE

WHAT IS FORREST GUMP'S PASSWORD?

1FORREST1.

CLINT EASTWOOD
OPENED A PRESCHOOL.

IT'S CALLED MAKE MY
DAY CARE CENTER.

WHAT CONCERT ONLY COSTS 45¢?

50 CENT FEATURING NICKELBACK.

DID YOU HEAR ABOUT THE ACTOR WHO BROKE HIS LEG ONSTAGE?

HE'S STILL IN THE CAST.

DID YOU HEAR THE TERMINATOR RETIRED?

NOW HE'S THE EXTERMINATOR.

WHY IS PETER PAN ALWAYS FLYING?

BECAUSE HE NEVERLANDS.

DID YOU GUYS SEE THE MOVIE ABOUT THE HOT DOG?

IT WAS AN OSCAR WIENER.

WHAT DO YOU CALL THE SECURITY GUARDS FOR SAMSUNG?

GUARDIANS OF THE GALAXY.

SINGING IN THE SHOWER IS PURE COMEDY UNTIL YOU GET SOAP IN YOUR MOUTH.

THEN IT'S A SOAP OPERA.

DAD: "SON, YOU CAN GO TO THE CONCERT, BUT NO CROWD-SURFING."

SON: "WHY?"

DAD: "BECAUSE YOU'LL JUST GET CARRIED AWAY."

MY SON STARTED A NEW BAND CALLED "BLANKET."

IT'S A COVER BAND.

JOHNNY CASH WAS KNOWN FOR PLAYING IN PRISONS.

HE LIKED TO HAVE A CAPTIVE AUDIENCE.

KID: "DAD, WHO IS YOUR FAVORITE DISNEY VILLAIN?"

DAD: "CAPTAIN HOOK. SINGLE-HANDEDLY."

I NEEDED A PASSWORD THAT WAS EIGHT CHARACTERS LONG, SO I PICKED *SNOW WHITE AND THE SEVEN DWARVES.*

I ONCE MET A SWEDE
WHO TOLD ME HE HATED
ALL MODERN MUSIC.

HE WAS BJORN IN THE
WRONG ERA.

THE SHOW MAY HAVE BEEN CALLED *SPONGEBOB SQUAREPANTS*, BUT PATRICK WAS THE REAL STAR.

I HAVE A PLAYLIST OF SONGS FROM EMINEM, THE CRANBERRIES, AND THE PEANUTS.

I NAMED IT THE TRAIL MIX.

HOW DO YOU WIN A FIGHT AGAINST THE ROCK?

PAPER.

I USED TO TELL A LOT OF POLITICAL JOKES.

BUT THEY JUST KEPT GETTING ELECTED TO OFFICE.

A SHEEP, A DRUM, AND A SNAKE FALL DOWN A CLIFF.

BAA-DUMM-TSS.

WHY DID VAN GOGH BECOME A PAINTER?

HE DIDN'T HAVE AN EAR FOR MUSIC.

MY FRIEND WANTS TO QUIT HIS JOB IN THE POSTAL SERVICE AND BECOME A COMEDIAN.

I DON'T THINK HIS DELIVERY IS GOOD ENOUGH.

WHY DIDN'T HANDEL GO SHOPPING?

BECAUSE HE WAS BAROQUE.

HOW MANY INDIE MUSIC CRITICS DOES IT TAKE TO CHANGE A LIGHT BULB?

IT'S AN OBSCURE NUMBER; YOU PROBABLY HAVEN'T HEARD IT.

DID YOU HEAR THEY'RE COMING OUT WITH THE FINAL BABE MOVIE?

IT'S CALLED *BABE 3: THE HONEYBAKED YEARS*.

WHAT'S A COWBOY'S FAVORITE PLACE TO LISTEN TO MUSIC?

THE O.K. CHORALE.

WHY DID MOZART GET
RID OF ALL HIS CHICKENS?

ALL THEY SAID WAS
"BACH, BACH, BACH."

WHAT COMPUTER IS MOST LIKELY TO WIN A GRAMMY?

A DELL.

WHAT DOES BILL GATES SAY WHEN HE FINISHES OFF A FREESTYLE RAP?

"WORD."

I'M KICKING MY SON OUT OF THE HOUSE BECAUSE HE'S OBSESSED WITH RAP.

I TOLD HIM TUPAC HIS BAGS AND LEAVE.

Chapter Four

PAR FOR THE TOUCHDOWN

WHY WAS THE COACH YELLING AT A VENDING MACHINE?

HE WANTED HIS QUARTER BACK.

WHAT'S THE HARDEST THING WHEN LEARNING TO SKATEBOARD?

THE CONCRETE.

HOW MANY GOLFERS DOES IT TAKE TO SCREW IN A LIGHT BULB?

FORE!

WHY DID THE BASKETBALL PLAYER BRING HIS SUITCASE TO THE GAME?

BECAUSE HE TRAVELED A LOT.

I COULDN'T FIGURE OUT WHY THE BASEBALL KEPT GETTING BIGGER.

THEN IT HIT ME.

DID YOU HEAR ABOUT
THE RUNNER WHO WAS AFRAID
OF HURDLES?

HE GOT OVER IT.

WHY WAS THE HUNTER ARRESTED WHILE MAKING BREAKFAST?

THE WARDEN FOUND OUT HE POACHED HIS EGGS.

WHAT DOES A SPRINTER EAT BEFORE A RACE?

NOTHING—THEY FAST.

WHERE DO BASKETBALL PLAYERS GO WHEN THEY NEED A UNIFORM?

NEW JERSEY.

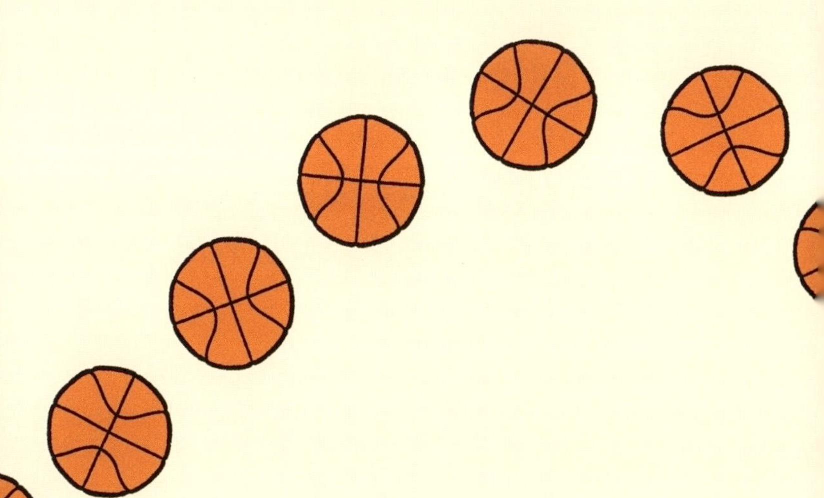

WHAT DO YOU CALL AN ANGRY BOW AND ARROW?

A CROSSBOW.

THE QUEEN OF ENGLAND WAS SO UPSET WITH HER POKER HAND THAT SHE THREW THE CARDS IN THE TOILET.

IT WAS A ROYAL FLUSH.

I COULDN'T QUITE
REMEMBER HOW TO THROW
A BOOMERANG.

EVENTUALLY,
IT CAME BACK TO ME.

WHY DID LEBRON LEAVE MIAMI?

HE COULDN'T STAND THE HEAT.

DID YOU HEAR ABOUT THE BOWLING ALLEY THAT HAD TO SHUT DOWN?

THE ENTIRE STAFF WENT ON STRIKE.

WHAT'S MIKE TYSON'S FAVORITE FOOD?

CORN. HE CAN EAT A WHOLE EAR.

WHAT DO YOU CALL A
NERVOUS JAVELIN PLAYER?

SHAKESPEARE.

WHAT IS A GOLF CLUB'S FAVORITE TYPE OF MUSIC?

SWING.

WHY WAS THE ICE CREAM CONE BAD AT TENNIS?

IT HAD A SOFT SERVE.

DAD: "I CAME IN SECOND PLACE AT TODAY'S HALF-MARATHON."

WIFE: "WHO WAS FIRST?"

DAD: "BEATS ME!"

I ALWAYS BRING EXTRA SOCKS WHEN I GO GOLFING.

YOU NEVER KNOW, I MIGHT GET A HOLE IN ONE!

WHY DID THE YOGURT CUP TURN UP ITS NOSE AT NASCAR?

IT WAS TOO CULTURED.

DID YOU HEAR THE JOKE ABOUT THE POP FLY?

I'D TELL YOU, BUT IT'LL GO WAY OVER YOUR HEAD.

MY FRIEND IS A
REALLY BAD BOWLER;
HE ALWAYS ENDS
UP IN THE GUTTER.

IT'S A STRIKING PROBLEM.

I TOLD MY WIFE I WAS
GOING TO JOIN A BOXING CLUB.

SHE SAID,
"KNOCK YOURSELF OUT."

MY SON'S AN
EXCELLENT GOLFER.

HE'S REALLY PUTT
TOGETHER ON THE GREENS.

WHY DID THE BASEBALL TEAM RECRUIT A CHEF?

THEY NEEDED A GOOD BATTER.

WHY WAS THE RECORD PLAYER DISQUALIFIED FROM THE RACE?

IT KEPT SKIPPING TRACKS.

D.A.D

Chapter 5

DADS ARE OUT OF THIS WORLD!

IF THE SILVER SURFER
AND IRON MAN TEAM UP,
THEY'D BE ALLOYS.

WHY DID THE GERM
CROSS THE MICROSCOPE?

TO GET TO THE
OTHER SLIDE.

WHAT'S THE MOST DETAIL-ORIENTED OCEAN?

THE PACIFIC.

R.I.P. BOILED WATER—
YOU WILL BE MIST.

WHY DID THE PHYSICIST AND THE BIOLOGIST BREAK UP?

BECAUSE THEY HAD NO CHEMISTRY.

WHAT DID THE GEOMETRY TEACHER SAY WHEN THE CLASS HAD TROUBLE SOLVING A PROBLEM?

"LET'S TRY A DIFFERENT ANGLE."

HOW DO YOU TELL A SCIENTIST THAT THEY HAVE BAD BREATH?

OFFER THEM AN EXPERI-MINT.

WHAT'S AN ASTRONAUT'S FAVORITE PART OF A COMPUTER?

THE SPACE BAR.

WHY DID THE PIECE
OF CANDY GO
TO OUTER SPACE?

TO FIND THE MILKY WAY.

KID: "DAD, CAN YOU EXPLAIN TO ME
WHAT A SOLAR ECLIPSE IS?"

DAD: "NO SUN."

I WAS GOING TO
TELL A SODIUM JOKE.

THEN I THOUGHT, Na.

DID YOU HEAR ABOUT
THE ARCHAEOLOGIST
WHO GOT FIRED?

HIS CAREER IS IN RUINS.

DID YOU HEAR ABOUT
THE CLEANERS WHO ALMOST
WENT TO SPACE?

THEY ENDED UP
SCRUBBING THE MISSION.

I TOLD A BAD CHEMISTRY JOKE ONCE.

IT GOT NO REACTION.

I'M STRUGGLING TO GET THROUGH THIS BOOK ON THE HISTORY OF GRAVITY.

IT'S REALLY WEIGHING ME DOWN.

WHY DO CATS HATE OUTER SPACE?

BECAUSE THEY DON'T LIKE VACUUMS.

HOW DO YOU GET
AN ASTRONAUT'S BABY
TO FALL ASLEEP?

YOU ROCKET.

WHY DIDN'T THE PHOTON HAVE ANY LUGGAGE?

IT'S TRAVELING LIGHT.

WHY WAS THE MOON
LOOKING FOR MORE MONEY?

IT WAS DOWN TO ITS
LAST QUARTER.

TWO BLOOD CELLS MET
AND FELL IN LOVE.

ALAS, IT WAS ALL IN VEIN.

DID YOU HEAR EINSTEIN DEVELOPED A THEORY ABOUT SPACE?

IT'S ABOUT TIME, TOO.

HOW MUCH DID THE NEUTRON COST?

NO CHARGE.

WHAT DO YOU CALL
THE INDECISIVE POWERHOUSE
OF THE CELL?

MIGHT-O-CHONDRIA.

WHY SHOULD YOU
TRUST YOUR CALCULATOR?

IT'S SOMETHING YOU
CAN COUNT ON.

WHAT'S A COMPUTER'S FAVORITE THING TO SNACK ON?

MICROCHIPS.

I DON'T KNOW THE DEFINITION OF THE WORD *APOCALYPSE*.

BUT I GUESS THAT'S NOT THE END OF THE WORLD.

WHY COULDN'T THE ASTRONAUT BOOK A HOTEL ON THE MOON?

BECAUSE IT WAS FULL.

WHY DIDN'T THE SUN
GO TO COLLEGE?

IT HAS ENOUGH DEGREES.

WHAT DO YOU CALL
A TICK ON THE MOON?

A LUNA TICK.

WHAT DID ONE TECTONIC
PLATE SAY WHEN IT BUMPED
NTO THE OTHER?

"MY FAULT!"

Chapter 6

DADS AND THEIR DEALS

I'M SO BROKE, I CAN'T
EVEN AFFORD
TO PAY ATTENTION.

KID: "I'M FREEZING. CAN WE TURN UP THE HEAT?"

DAD: "GO STAND IN THE CORNER OF THE ROOM. THEN YOU'LL FEEL BETTER."

KID: "WHY?"

DAD: "BECAUSE A CORNER IS 90 DEGREES."

A NICKEL AND DIME
WERE WALKING ACROSS
A BRIDGE AND THE
NICKEL JUMPED OFF.
WHY DIDN'T THE DIME?

IT HAD MORE CENTS.

WHY DOES IT COST SO MUCH TO PUT AIR IN A TIRE?

INFLATION.

DID YOU HEAR ABOUT
THE ROBBERY THAT TOOK PLACE
ON BLACK FRIDAY?

IT WAS A REAL STEAL!

WHY DID THE CASHIER RIP MONEY IN HALF?

THEY WERE ASKED TO BREAK A BILL.

WHERE DO BIRDS STAY WHEN THEY TRAVEL?

SOMEPLACE CHEEP.

WHY DID THE MAN BRING HIS WATCH TO THE BANK?

HE WANTED TO SAVE TIME.

HOW CAN YOU DOUBLE YOUR MONEY?

BY FOLDING IT IN HALF.

WHAT DOES SANTA CALL HIS WIFE DURING TAX SEASON?

A DEPENDENT CLAUS.

HOW DOES THE
VATICAN PAY ITS BILLS?

THEY USE PAPAL.

HOW IS MY WALLET
LIKE AN ONION?

EVERY TIME I OPEN IT, I CRY.

I USED TO BE A SUCCESSFUL BANKER.

THEN I LOST INTEREST.

PEOPLE ASK WHY I ALWAYS KEEP AN EMERGENCY TWENTY-DOLLAR BILL IN THE POCKET OF MY RAINCOAT.

I'M JUST SAVING IT FOR A RAINY DAY.

KID: "GEE, DAD, THANKS FOR TURNING DOWN THE THERMOSTAT."

DAD: "DON'T SWEAT IT."

I JUST FOUND A NICKEL ON THE GROUND, AND I HAVE A FEELING I WILL FIND A PENNY LATER.

IT'S MY SIXTH SENSE.

THE ELECTRIC COMPANY CALLED TODAY TO TELL ME MY PAYMENT WAS OUTSTANDING.

WHAT A NICE COMPLIMENT.

I COULDN'T BELIEVE
IT STARTED RAINING DIMES AND
QUARTERS YESTERDAY.

THAT WAS QUITE THE CHANGE
IN THE WEATHER.

WHAT DO YOU CALL ONE HUNDRED CENTIPEDES?

A DOLLARPEDE.

I'M SICK AND TIRED OF MY WIFE RUNNING THE LAWN SPRINKLERS CONSTANTLY AND WASTING MONEY.

IT'S REALLY IRRIGATING.

HOW DO YOU HANDLE
A BULL THAT'S
CONSTANTLY CHARGING?

YOU JUST TAKE AWAY
HIS CREDIT CARD.

MY WIFE AND I ORDERED
DUCK FOR DINNER LAST NIGHT.

THE BILL WAS HUGE!

I HAD A WHOLE PLAN
FOR HOW TO SAVE MONEY
ON THE DEEP-FRIED
TURKEY THIS THANKSGIVING.

BUT THE IDEA REALLY BLEW
UP IN MY FACE.

WHY DID THE DJ
BECOME POOR FROM PLAYING
THE STOCK MARKET?

BECAUSE HE LOVED
MASSIVE DROPS.

KID: "DAD, CAN I GO TO THE IMAGINE DRAGONS CONCERT? TICKETS ARE $100."

DAD: "WOW, IMAGINING DRAGONS HAS GOTTEN A LOT MORE EXPENSIVE SINCE I WAS A KID."

MY DAUGHTERS ASKED
IF THEY COULD GO TO THE
TAYLOR CONCERT.

WHEN I FOUND
OUT THE PRICE, MY ANSWER
WAS A SWIFT NO.

WHY ARE PIGGY
BANKS SO WISE?

THEY'RE FILLED WITH
COMMON CENTS.

MY WIFE ALWAYS SAYS
I'M NOT GENEROUS ENOUGH.
SO I GAVE AWAY ALL
MY BATTERIES TODAY,
FREE OF CHARGE.

MY WIFE SAID IF I DIDN'T STOP TRYING TO SAVE MONEY ON THE AC BILL, SHE WAS GOING TO MOVE TO HAWAII.

I SAID, "ALL RIGHT, ALL RIGHT, I'LL SET IT TO ALOHA TEMPERATURE."

MY GRANDFATHER INVENTED THE REARVIEW MIRROR. HE MADE MILLIONS, AND HE'S NEVER LOOKED BACK SINCE!

I WON $3 MILLION IN THE LOTTERY THIS WEEKEND, SO I DECIDED TO DONATE A QUARTER TO CHARITY. NOW I HAVE $2,999,999.75.

Chapter 7

SUSPENDERS, HIGH SOCKS, TIES, AND OTHER DAD LOOKS

WHAT DO YOU CALL A BELT MADE OF WATCHES?

A WAIST OF TIME.

WHAT DID THE POLICEMAN SAY TO HIS BELLY BUTTON?

"YOU'RE UNDER A VEST!"

WHY DOES WALDO
ALWAYS WEAR STRIPES?

HE'S AFRAID
OF BEING SPOTTED.

WHAT'S THE DIFFERENCE
BETWEEN A POORLY DRESSED
MAN ON A TRICYCLE AND A
WELL-DRESSED MAN ON A BICYCLE?

ATTIRE.

I DIDN'T LIKE HAVING
A MUSTACHE AT FIRST,
BUT IT'S GROWING ON ME.

WHY DO SWEATERS PREFER TO HANG OUT TOGETHER?

THEY'RE PRETTY CLOSE-KNIT.

DID YOU HEAR ABOUT
THE FIRE AT THE SHOE FACTORY?

MANY SOLES WERE LOST.

YESTERDAY, MY WIFE
LOOKED AT MY OUTFIT AND SAID
I MUST BE COLOR-BLIND.

THAT REALLY CAME OUT
OF THE ORANGE.

WHO WON THE
NECK-DECORATING CONTEST?

IT WAS A TIE.

MY WIFE ASKED ME TO
WEAR SCOTTISH ATTIRE.

I REALLY KILT IT.

I'VE DECIDED TO THROW OUT THE SOCKS I'M WEARING.

THEY'RE ON THEIR LAST LEGS.

MY TAILOR IS HAPPY TO MAKE
A PAIR OF PANTS FOR ME.

OR AT LEAST SEW IT SEAMS.

MY FAVORITE NAVY SPORT
COAT GOT A TEAR IN IT.

I GUESS YOU COULD SAY IT
WASN'T MY STRONG SUIT.

WHEN I'M STRESSED, I LIKE TO IRON CLOTHES.

IT'S A GREAT WAY TO LET OFF STEAM.

MY NEW SWEATER HAD
A PROBLEM WITH STATIC,
SO I RETURNED IT.

I DEMANDED THE STORE
GIVE ME A NEW
ONE FREE OF CHARGE.

I WENT TO A TOBACCO SHOP ONLY TO DISCOVER THAT IT HAD BEEN REPLACED BY AN APPAREL STORE.

CLOTHES BUT NO CIGAR.

WHAT DID DAD SAY
AFTER HE TRIPPED AT THE
LABOR DAY BARBECUE?

"DON'T WORRY, I'M ALL WHITE!"

WHY WAS THE BELT
SENT TO JAIL?

FOR HOLDING UP
A PAIR OF PANTS.

WHY DID THE SOCK REFUSE TO GO ON A DATE?

IT HAD COLD FEET.

MY SON OPENED A BUSINESS SHOWING FOLKS HOW TO TIE BOW TIES.

IT'S A KNOT-FOR-PROFIT.

I TOLD MY SWEATER
ABOUT MY PROBLEMS, AND
NOW IT'S UNRAVELING.

MY WIFE HIT THE CEILING
WHEN I CAME
DOWNSTAIRS FOR OUR DATE.

SHE SAID I HAD SOME
WARDROBE ISSUES I NEEDED
TO IRON OUT.

WHEN I WAS A BOY, I WORKED AT A SHIRT FACTORY.

IT PAID WELL, BUT THE COMPANY CULTURE WAS SEW-SEW.

MY COWBOY BOOTS ARE ON SABBATICAL.

THEY NEEDED TO DO SOME SOLE SEARCHING.

MY DAUGHTER BROUGHT ALL HER LIPSTICK AND EYE SHADOW TO SCHOOL YESTERDAY.

APPARENTLY, SHE HAD A MAKEUP EXAM.

MY FAVORITE WAY TO DRESS IS IN ALL BLACK.

MY FASHION SENSE IS SECOND TO NUN.

WHAT DO YOU CALL A STYLISH VEGETABLE?

A CHIC-ORY.

I LEFT THE FABRIC STORE
AFTER SEEING THE PRICES.

I REFUSE TO BE FLEECED.

MY WIFE TOLD ME I NEEDED
TO ELEVATE MY WARDROBE,
SO I BOUGHT A PAIR
OF PLATFORM SNEAKERS.

I'M ALWAYS TRYING TO REACH
NEW HEIGHTS IN FASHION.

MY WIFE SAID I SHOULD BE PUTTING ON A NEW PAIR OF SOCKS EVERY DAY.

BY THE END OF THE WEEK, I COULDN'T GET MY SHOES ON.

MY WIFE HAS A CLOSET
FULL OF DESIGNER
HEELS AND FLATS.

I TRY TO BE SUPPORTIVE
AND ENCOURAGE HER TO
PER-SHOE HER DREAMS.

Beer

Chapter 8

BEER AND BEERY BAD HUMOR

WHAT IS BEER'S
FAVORITE GAME?

HOPSCOTCH!

WHAT IS CASPER
THE FRIENDLY GHOST'S
FAVORITE BEER?

A PALE ALE.

I QUIT DRINKING FOR GOOD.

NOW, I DRINK FOR EVIL.

I AM GOING TO A NEW GYM CALLED "RESOLUTIONS." IT HAS EXERCISE EQUIPMENT FOR THE FIRST TWO WEEKS OF THE YEAR AND THEN TURNS INTO A BAR FOR THE REST OF IT.

WHAT DO OLD PEOPLE
CALL HAPPY HOUR?

NAP TIME.

THE BEACH BOYS
WALK INTO A BAR.

"ROUND?"

"ROUND."

"GET A ROUND?"

"I'LL GET A ROUND!"

WHAT DID THE
BIG BEER NAME ITS BABY?

MICROBREW.

HOW DO YOU
MAKE BUDWEISER?

SEND HIM TO SCHOOL.

WHY AREN'T DOGS ALLOWED IN BARS?

BECAUSE THEY CAN'T CONTROL THEIR LICKER!

I GOT CARDED AT A LIQUOR STORE, AND MY BLOCKBUSTER CARD FELL OUT.

THE CASHIER SAID, "NEVER MIND."

DID YOU HEAR ABOUT THE RABBIT WHO WORKS AT THE LOCAL MICROBREWERY?

HE'S IN CHARGE OF THE HOPS.

MARVIN GAYE USED
TO KEEP A SHEEP
AT HIS VINEYARD.

HE LIKED TO
HERD IT THROUGH THE
GRAPEVINE.

I INSTALLED A BAR ON
MY ROOF THE OTHER DAY.

DRINKS ARE ON THE HOUSE!

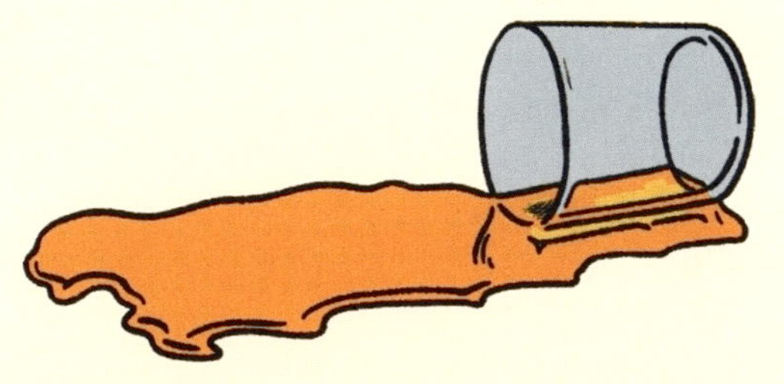

YOU KNOW WHAT'S REALLY NEAT?

ORDERING A WHISKEY WITH NO ICE.

FOR OUR WEDDING, MY WIFE AND I DECIDED TO OPEN A FEW BOTTLES FROM MY LATE GRANDFATHER'S WHISKEY COLLECTION.

HE WAS THERE IN SPIRIT.

DID YOU HEAR THAT TOM CRUISE RECENTLY INVESTED IN A NEW LIQUOR COMPANY?

IT WILL BE CALLED "WHISKEY BUSINESS."

MY FRIEND THINKS
BARTENDERS ARE
BORING, BUT I FIND THEM
INTOXICATING.

IMAGINE YOU WALK INTO
A BAR AND THERE IS A
LONG LINE OF PEOPLE WAITING
TO TAKE A SWING AT YOU.

THAT'S THE PUNCH LINE.

A NEUTRON WALKED INTO A BAR AND ASKED HOW MUCH IT WOULD COST FOR A BEER.

THE BARTENDER REPLIED, “FOR YOU, NO CHARGE.”

WHAT IS THE DIFFERENCE BETWEEN BEER AND PEE?

ABOUT THIRTY MINUTES.

WHAT DO DAD JOKES AND WINE HAVE IN COMMON?

THEY ONLY GET BETTER WITH AGE!

WHY DID THE WHISKEY SOUR BREAK UP WITH THE MARGARITA?

THE MARGARITA WAS JUST TOO SALTY.

A PAIR OF JUMPER CABLES WALKED INTO A BAR. THE BARTENDER SAID, "I'LL SERVE YOU, BUT DON'T START ANYTHING!"

A NOSE WALKED INTO A BAR AND ASKED FOR A DRINK. THE BARTENDER SAID, "SORRY, I CAN'T SERVE YOU. YOU'RE ALREADY OFF YOUR FACE."

A HAMBURGER WALKED
INTO A BAR. THE BARTENDER SAID,
"SORRY, WE DON'T SERVE FOOD."

I OPENED A NEW BAR,
AND WE HAVE AN
OPEN-DOOR POLICY.

SHOW UP WITH BEER,
AND WE'LL
OPEN THE DOOR.

DID YOU HEAR ABOUT THE DRAFT-DODGING GRAPE?

UNFORTUNATELY FOR HIM, HE WAS EVENTUALLY PRESSED INTO SERVICE.

THE WAITER LAST NIGHT ASSURED ME THAT THE NONALCOHOLIC WINE ON THE MENU WAS DELICIOUS.

I TOLD HIM HE HAD NO PROOF.

MY WIFE'S A REAL WINE ENTHUSIAST. THE MORE WINE SHE DRINKS, THE MORE ENTHUSIASTIC SHE GETS.

DO LIBRARIANS PREFER WHITE WINE?

NO, THEY LIKE THEIRS WELL RED.

LAST NIGHT, I WAS HAVING WINE WITH MY WIFE WHEN SHE SAID, "I LOVE YOU SO MUCH, YOU KNOW."

I ASKED HER, "IS THAT YOU OR THE WINE TALKING?"

SHE SAID, "IT'S ME TALKING TO THE WINE."

MY WIFE AND I WERE SHARING A BOTTLE OF WINE LAST NIGHT WHEN I STARTED COMPLAINING.

SHE TOLD ME TO PUT A CORK IN IT.

STOP
STOP
STOP
STOP
STOP
STOP
STOP
STOP

Chapter 9

WHAT HAS FOUR WHEELS AND IS DRIVEN BY A DAD?

TELL ME A JOKE
ABOUT A FLAT TIRE.

NO PRESSURE.

WHEN IS A CAR NOT A CAR?

WHEN IT TURNS
INTO A DRIVEWAY.

WHAT ADVICE DID THE THERAPIST
GIVE THE SEMITRAILER?

TO KEEP ON TRUCKING.

WHAT KIND OF NOISE DOES A WITCH'S VEHICLE MAKE?

BRRRROOOOM, BRRRROOOOM.

WHAT KIND OF CAR DOES
A SHEEP LIKE TO DRIVE?

A *LAMB*ORGHINI.

DAD, WHEN HE PUTS THE CAR IN REVERSE:

"AH, THIS TAKES ME BACK."

I'M SELLING MY USED TAXI.

IT'S IN FARE CONDITION.

MY FRIEND DROVE HIS EXPENSIVE CAR INTO A TREE AND FOUND OUT MERCEDES BENDS.

WHAT DO YOU CALL AN AIRPLANE WITH NO DECORATION OR BRANDING?

A PLAIN.

I RECENTLY BOUGHT A CAR
WITH A BROKEN REVERSE GEAR.

THERE'S NO GOING BACK NOW.

THE NEW CEO OF HONDA WAS TOLD HE HAD TO RESIGN HIS POSITION OR BE FIRED.

HE DECIDED TO LEAVE OF HIS OWN ACCORD.

WHY DID THE SAILBOAT START SMOKING?

PIER PRESSURE.

I DON'T LIKE WEARING SEAT BELTS, BUT AFTER A LOT OF PRESSURE FROM MY FAMILY, I FINALLY BUCKLED.

I PITCHED A SITCOM ABOUT AIRPLANES TO A TV NETWORK, BUT IT DIDN'T GET PICKED UP.

THEY SAID IT HAD A BAD PILOT.

I SPENT $500 ON A LIMO FOR MY DAUGHTER'S PROM, AND IT DIDN'T EVEN COME WITH A LIMO DRIVER.

ALL THAT MONEY SPENT AND NOTHING TO CHAUFFER IT.

WHILE LEARNING TO DRIVE,
MY SON MADE A WRONG TURN INTO
THE CEMETERY PARKING LOT.
I TOLD HIM,

"STOP, THAT'S A DEAD END."

I'VE BEEN HIT BY THE SAME BIKE THREE TIMES THIS WEEK.

IT'S A VICIOUS CYCLE.

MY WIFE ALWAYS WANTS ME TO DRIVE THE JEEP WHEN SHE GOES OUT WITH FRIENDS. THAT WAY, I CAN WRANGLER HOME AFTERWARD.

THE INVENTION OF
THE WHEEL?

NOW, THAT REALLY GOT
THINGS ROLLING!

HOW DO YOU KNOW WHEN A WHEEL IS OUT OF SHAPE?

IT WILL TIRE EASILY.

WHAT HAS FOUR WHEELS AND FLIES?

A GARBAGE TRUCK.

I HAVE A FRIEND WHO DRIVES A STEAMROLLER.

HE'S SUCH A FLATTERER.

WHAT DID THE FORD SAY TO THE TESLA WHEN IT HAD A BAD ODOR EMANATING FROM ITS ENGINE?

"YOU HAVE A STRONG MUSK!"

WHAT DO YOU CALL A FORD FIESTA THAT RUNS OUT OF GAS?

A FORD SIESTA.

WHY ARE PISTONS SUCH
BAD EMPLOYEES?

THEY ONLY WORK
AFTER THEY'RE FIRED.

MY WIFE ASKED ME IF I COULD GO WASH THE CAR WITH OUR SON.

I TOLD HER A HOSE WOULD PROBABLY BE MORE EFFICIENT.

ON OUR WAY TO THE HOSPITAL,
MY WIFE GAVE BIRTH TO
OUR SON IN THE CAR.

WE NAMED HIM "CARSON."

I WAS REALLY STOKED ABOUT BUYING ONE OF THOSE NEW ELECTRIC CARS.

BUT WHEN I GOT TO THE DEALERSHIP, THE PRICES WERE JUST TOO SHOCKING!

HOW DO YOU STOP YOUR
TEEN FROM TEXTING AND DRIVING?

BUY HIM A FORD FOCUS.

Chapter 10

DADS NAILING IT

DID YOU HEAR THAT THE CEO OF IKEA WAS RECENTLY ELECTED PRIME MINISTER OF SWEDEN?

HE'S NOW BUSY ASSEMBLING HIS CABINET.

WHAT DID ONE FURNITURE MAKER SAY TO ANOTHER DURING A TENSE DISCUSSION?

"LET'S TABLE THIS."

WHY WAS THE AXE SUCH AN IMPORTANT INVENTION AT THE TIME?

THE TECHNOLOGY WAS CUTTING-EDGE.

I GAVE THE HANDYMAN A TO-DO LIST, BUT HE ONLY DID JOBS 1, 3, AND 5.

TURNS OUT HE ONLY DOES ODD JOBS.

WHAT WAS IT LIKE BEFORE THE CROWBAR WAS INVENTED?

CROWS DRANK AT HOME.

THE OLD CARPENTER ALWAYS NAILED IT, BUT THE NEW GUY JUST SCREWS EVERYTHING UP.

WHAT DID THE HAMMER SAY TO THE NAIL?

"LET'S FIND YOU A STUD!"

WHAT DID THE METAL WASHER SAY TO THE BOLT?

"STOP TURNING ON ME."

WHY DID THE SAW ALWAYS GET INVITED TO PARTIES?

IT KNEW HOW TO CUT LOOSE!

THIS WRENCH REALLY HAS A WAY OF TURNING THINGS AROUND.

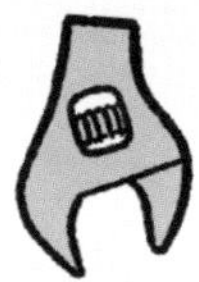

A TRUSTY LADDER ALWAYS STEPS UP WHEN YOU NEED IT.

WHY DID THE HAMMER CALL THE CROWBAR NOSY?

BECAUSE IT'S CONSTANTLY PRYING INTO THINGS.

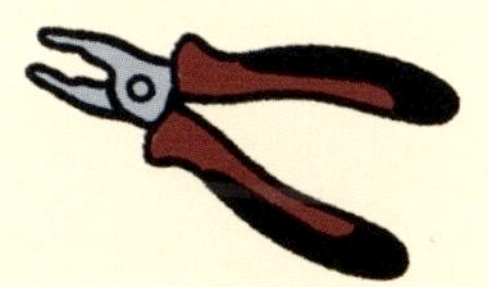

WHY DID THE PLIERS TAKE A DAY OFF?

THEY NEEDED TO GET A GRIP.

WHY DO ALL THE OTHER TOOLS DISLIKE SANDPAPER?

IT'S A BIT ROUGH AROUND THE EDGES.

WHY WAS THE DRILL NEVER INVITED TO PARTIES?

IT WAS A REAL BORE.

WHY DID THE POWER DRILL GET PROMOTED?

IT WAS ALWAYS BORING INTO THE TASK.

I ASKED MY JIGSAW FOR ADVICE, BUT IT JUST KEPT CUTTING ME OFF.

DAD 1: "YOUR GRASS ALWAYS LOOKS REALLY GREAT EVERY YEAR."

DAD 2: "THANKS. IT DEFINITELY HAS GOOD LAWNGEVITY."

MOWING THE LAWN NEVER GETS OLD;
IT JUST KEEPS GROWING ON ME.

HOW DO YOU HAVE
CUTTING-EDGE LAWN CARE?

SHEAR EFFORT.

WE'RE LEARNING MORE AND MORE ABOUT LAWN CARE WITH EACH PASSING YEAR.

IT'S REALLY A GROWING FIELD.

WHAT DO YOU CALL A LAWN THAT RISES FROM THE DEAD?

BLADES OF GLORY.

WHO'S THE BIGGEST TOOL IN THE OCEAN?

THE HAMMERHEAD SHARK.

WHEN I GOT BACK FROM HOME DEPOT, MY WIFE ASKED, "WHAT DID YOU BUY, JOHN, DEAR?"

I SAID, "NAH, I WENT WITH KUBOTA."

THE POWER DRILL
WAS AN ABSOLUTELY
REVOLUTIONARY IDEA.

WHILE DOING YARD WORK YESTERDAY, I GOT IN A FIGHT WITH MY PICKAX.

IT PICKED ME APART.

WHAT'S THE BEST WAY TO CARVE WOOD?

WHITTLE BY WHITTLE.

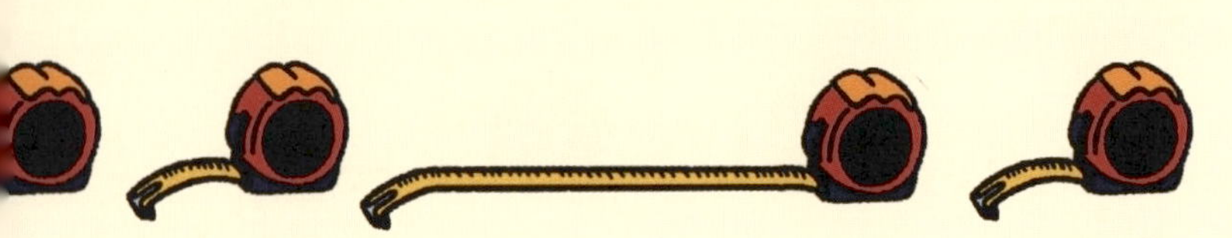

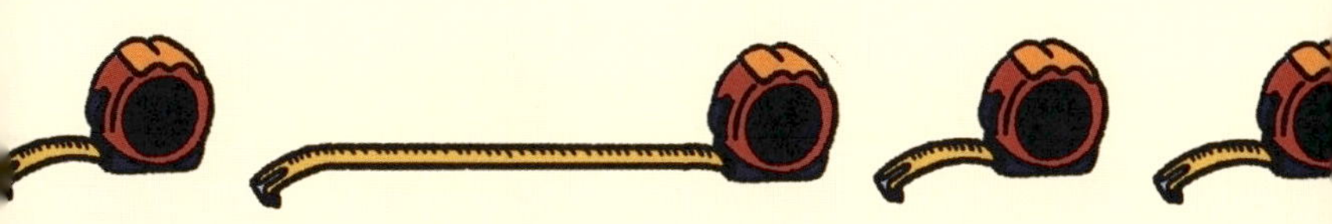

I WANTED TO TELL
YOU A CONSTRUCTION JOKE, BUT
I'M STILL WORKING ON IT.

Thank you to Hudson and Suzana, who can tell a bad joke with the worst of 'em. Thank you to Maria Ribas at Stonesong for bringing this book to life and for believing in the power of a truly stinky joke. Thank you to Jarrett Dieterle, whose detailed and diligent editorial work made this much badness possible.

An extra big thank you to Olivia Roberts for the many bad jokes along the way. Thank you for understanding this project, shaping it to be infinitely better/worse, and making the whole process plenty of cringeworthy fun. Major finger guns of gratitude to Maggie Edelman for the spiffy and spot-on design.

And thank you to the entire team at Chronicle Books, whose talent and thoughtfulness has made this book much more than the sum of its jokes.